Birth Center in Corporate Woods

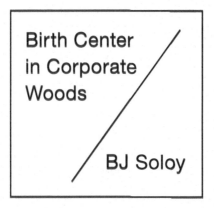

Birth Center in Corporate Woods

BJ Soloy

Black Lawrence Press

Black Lawrence Press

Executive Editor: Diane Goettel
Book Cover and Interior Design: Zoe Norvell

Front Cover Artwork:
"…another nothing…" by Sean Semones
Acrylic, ink, and graphite on wood panel
2021
24" x 18"

ISBN: 978-1-62557-155-7

Published 2025 by Black Lawrence Press.
Printed in the United States.

for

Julien—

You really   *are*   *such a*

pretty one...

and

Lucien Rabbit—

...let the towns drift slowly by

TABLE OF
CONTENTS

YET MUSIC

REMISSION INVENTORY

THE SINGING EAR

YET
MUSIC

BACK ON
CENTRAL ST.,
MAGNITUDE
EXPLAINED

It's the season of not wanting to get out of bed.
It's also Chevy Truck Month. You're in another town

where the air tastes like Christ's return & Round-Up

while I'm writing you from back home, of course, where
it always looks like rain. The wolves in my dream

let me know what was coming, but I still shiver
as it comes through the door. Long story long,

we extract ourselves by landing in what
the church basement Folger-breath alcoholics

call bottom. A magic trick, this day's wind
coming through & I'm always here, a basement

in tornado season. The four chambers of my core are:
two themed restaurants, two themed hotel rooms. I'm art

on the wall of the oncologist's office. With the present
season already pickled & otherwise enfeebled, I clap

my lids together to regather. Gather around me,
predictable, summonable darkness. Introduce yourself.

Just this last Friday I found myself wearing out the highway,
passed by trucks full of boar semen & petroleum & sand

& families. I was born on a Friday too hot, breached through
a cut made too calm, my forehead or my heel the first to debut.

Then the hours of the day changed. Then the weather
ate itself. I let myself outside to wallow. Outside, all I know

is this triptych of billboards crowning the Walgreens.
In the wind & dark, it is so like a Gerhard Richter triptych

that I have to toss half a cigarette to come inside & find a book
I knew had Richter—whose name I, sadly, couldn't recall—

in its index. The wind takes the surfaces & makes them texture.
If I were to tell you it's spring, I'd be lying to get you to conjure

a certain brand of light. If I were to perform this in pearl buttons
& my Montana boots, it's just to conjure the five fingers of whiskey

& fourteen hands of horse of a motif. I imagine I'll die on a Friday,
but who can guess what days will be left? Who can hear in this heat

or memory of heat? "Be careful," this stranger in a dress
says to Cindy at Chez Charlie. "'Be careful,' she says," says Cindy

at Chez Charlie, walking to the parking lot. For a minute,
this stranger in a dress is my mother & my mother is lost

& just staring at me. I won't look away. Our eyes
are a subscription neither of us will cancel & every morning

will be a lonely lawn waiting for the news to land.
When I was younger, I almost pushed a friend, Dave,

off a cliff. It was a joke a foot from horror. This has been
my entire adult relationship with myself. Dave's cousin, Paul,

comes to town & reminds me that, twenty years ago, he jumped
out of our upstairs bathroom window. Swithened, the tree,

already dead, catches fire proper. Earlier this afternoon, as I was
feeding wiggling roaches pinched in my fingers to a dry

old lizard, I thought of communion & the desert & the numbers
forty & forty & temptation & sacrificing quarters to machines.

Lately I'm always drinking old, cold coffee or cooled, once-hot tea.
I'm slowly digging this hole in my forehead. It started an old spot,

a dry button, but it'll end up a Sergio Leone horn section
with strings! I can't stop picking at it & it can't stop singing.

Twenty years ago, Paul came in the front door looking shaken,
both rattled & calmed by gravity. Oh, stupid Calm, you can touch

my hand but won't hold onto me as I undo. It's the difference
between plucking an eyebrow & plucking an eye. Whatever

that was—a drill, a frustrated raptor, a revving engine, an alarm
—suddenly quiets. I stop. I hear the parade. Bill Callahan says,

through his gilded gutter, "I used to be sort of blind; / Now
I ca-a-a-an sort of see." Stupid Calm, I needed you to blind me.

[INDISTINGUISHABLE
CHATTER]

Years later, I find myself empty & at bottom—tossed into a dry well
& seeing the night sky

at one & one-half hours past noon. Years later, I'm passing through
Des Moines like a kidney stone.

Years earlier, I slept in the basement.
We had mice, lonely as the three songs Mom knew on piano.

Years later, you sit in my boxers
on the couch, cuter than a mouse turd. Our dog-faced boy stinks

beside you, a pillow of twitching sleep. If I died tomorrow, what would
   you sing for my funeral songs?

I don't have a real suit; what would you burn me in? Place me in the
garden & face me toward the sun or brightest object

around. Years earlier, when the sun
was worth talking about,

I could sell my shadow by the foot. The first time

we slept by each other, after sleeping together for the first time, I only
had these two old pillows,

always an abundance, & I gave them both to you. Julie, I didn't sleep at
all that night. Years later,

you're freezing in your sleeping bag. I look
up at stars & have no idea what to look at. It's like looking at

the stock market
or the panic in your eyes.

The man who sells us firewood on the Missouri border has a voice very
rough, but very sweet—

the voice of a retired dominatrix with pneumonia whose hand I'm
holding with both of my own. Our dog-faced boy

snores & gnats gather 'round his junk as if it's all
a holy river in cancer season. At this point, we're just burning

the rest because we have it.

THIS TELEVISION SHOW
IS IMPLICITLY SUBTITLED
"THE DESTRUCTION

of the American Family." This one's commercials are occasionally
interrupted by heartfelt moments of personal disclosure.

I have this prosthetic hand I use to hold my own hand. Perfect circle.

Restless in your alarm clock's unreadable red,
you bury yourself back into the circular night I apparently engender. I
    do not drink milk

for I am no longer an infant. Window open,
window closed, I alternate. Sometimes there are paintings on the walls,
    sometimes

photographs. I do not drink milk; I drink champagne. Soon after I
marry the Eads Bridge, I marry

the Ford Aerostar, the shed on Blendon Place, this empty rest stop.
If you're not sure which way

a product is supposed to face
when operating, face the project's registered name toward you.

Just at that ditch
people drown each other in

.

between reading in bed & sleeping in bed, I can't tell
where oscillating fan & compressed human breath split or share.

This television show is subtitled "In the background
of the photograph is another person taking a photograph, so get over
    yourself,

you sad little fuck desperately guarding your own idiosyncrasies."

Mothers stop producing milk. Wolf Blitzer keeps a straight face. An
ugly baby on the bus sleeps under this last, smug weather.

I swear by the stalactites of designer brand off-white paint
frozen on the ceiling, your crystallization

on my unshaven chin. I swear by the antibiotics in our meat that this is limited time only.

BUT LITTLE
TO SAY

At Chez Charlie the jukebox doesn't change
but it's free. Hours pass in a montage of me

seated all drawn in as if bracing for contact—
a tree just before timbered across the choking

creek, a bridge out, or a mucilage needing this all
to connect. Montage ends with my naked

lonely legs & our fridge's naked lonely light.
I've never been the same. My face slacks

from this day-long process of falling asleep.
I collapse in bed & sleep comes short-lived

as screaming cat sex, yowls solid as crystal
breaking under the dumpster. Never

been the same. All the lights go out at once.
You get out of the hospital & we get a new cat

& she never shuts up & you love her something
stupid. At Chez Charlie, there's a coffee cup

named Uncle Joe for the funeral fund of a day
-time regular. Custer shoots his own horse

through the head. The landscape slows
& reddens. Spreads as if the snow itself

is wounded. Tourists, if you see a hill, climb it
or at least name it. Back door opens & closes,

no one comes in, the freezer starts to sound
like dogs fighting. We are not a good people.

MY FACE IS A WRINKLED KNUCKLE, REALIZING LAMENTATIONS HAS BEEN REMOVED FROM OUR TEXT

You say it's surely fall, for all the animals
are either fat or dying, but the autumn scene

is saccharine. Genuinely terrifying. To be pitted,
pruned, & jellied.   To be sung at.

Wait, is that the Franklin Hotel's fire alarm or a chorus?
A scream?

One can't smoke in this building, but child
sacrifice is apparently de rigueur. White girls

karaoke Bon Jovi into the void
of Strawberry Point, Iowa

& no one dies completely,

but time's passage thickens & tonight's now
an obstructed bowel, necrotic tissue spreading

like bruise-blue outward from the sunset.

An epigraph from Mitski or John Cage
or Laurie Anderson might frame it easier

but they're all dead or won't speak to me, etc.

& each night is only oh so long. You've a hard time
making sense of today. Lights up, lights down,

& here you are. 364 more of these & you get a candle.

TO BE SUNG
IN THE LANGUAGE
OF THE AUDIENCE

Back in St. Louis, I'm taking my time
on a nostalgia tour of blind love
& misery. I'm many different moments.

I'm trapped in some forsaken munitions depot
eating dollar bills. I'm watching the river—
indeed, a thing that's sung of, & dirty.

I think of an octogenarian eating mac n' cheese.
Blowing on it. When Angel was murdered,
I went to my room in Dogtown & listened

to "Sue's Last Ride" on repeat until I'd vacated
myself & could tell someone else. I miss her. I get
the shower as hot as I can. There were elections

yesterday. Tommy got his fiddle stolen
while delivering pizzas & died four years later.
Maybe suicide? HIV? Overdose? The trinity?

Nobody tells me anything. Who are we? Buy
a snow shovel & some serious boots & an economy
pack of lighters & you'll feel ready. The east eventually

becomes the west, but there is no night anymore. If
you call me by my real name, I'll disappear. Onebody.
Ashcan. The industrial west in amber, full

of yesterday's weather. As your mom's parents
warned her of being Ted Bundy's type, my mom
was getting over rheumatic fever by buying

a $100 Yamaha guitar that is still my favorite thing.
Forty-five years pass & Guy Fieri is eating beef
with his fingers & then licking his beefened fingertips,

saying, "Keep that beef nice & moist,"
& I'm instantly pregnant. Twins. My tethered
ventricles cough, full of rhythm & echo

as a sump pump. Tom Petty's heart is dead. Prince's. Still.
Radar shows purple settling in on Topeka, slow
& loud as a Medicare commercial. A name

-brand set of smiles. We're smiling.
We're not getting any better. I miss some things
I cannot name. Written of November, but

not in November, this is now lying to you. This November
morning, the winter sky at first light is whiter than a baby
on an anti-abortion billboard in mid-state Missouri.

Slow & strange as an eephus, zoom out further.
Pinhole. Clap your hands. The fuzz in the air.
The heroes & perverts of high school mythomania

are in a Budget rent-a-truck on some even-
numbered highway, but don't parole
your lesser iteration, your serial self's

least popular spin-off. Kill it off.
Wrapped in plastic. It is performatively impossible
to tickle oneself or follow one's own advice.

                    Someone—right now—
is a witness on the highway: the halves of deer;
the Lion's Den, live dancers. Someone is deciding

to move to Little Rock, Arkansas. Someone else
leaves their husband, skin, their anchor
of obligation. As such, suckle the serif

off this poster. Take a nap. Let's meet
in the Green Room, the rest room, a boom town,
the zoo. We won't be here long.

I KNEW BEFORE I STARTED
THAT I WOULD END UP
A BODY IN THE FIELDS

Our infant son attempts
to nurse from me, but I am dry
as a ghost town well. I am useless, walking
a circuit: the table, the kitchen, the front door.
I'm a soft city boy, a Missouri muffin.
What's the over-under on that piano
being in tune? Penelope Fitzgerald,
The Beginning of Spring: "Middle-aged poets,
middle-aged parents, have no defenses."
Don't be sorrow. This is not a conversation.

One lives one's life & tries, really, but still finds one's self
on Bass Pro Drive in Independence, MO,
as if this landscape were accident. Good
is the opposite of this good. As if a bad
cup of coffee can wake it all up.
The old men cosplaying retirement talk
Martin Marietta. Dollar General. As if
this accident were accident. Bad morning
music, I look a mess. The sky looks for sale.

WORLD WAR
DRONE WARDROBE

When one breaks their toes, one tapes them together
& walks slowly, slowly, Amazon Prime trucks
tearing hell through the intersection. Another dream:

Seventy-three years ago, a woman in a dress
takes aim. Important instructions to follow. Another:

I'm on death row, a theme I attribute
to Cath-o-lic school. Ratified by the miserable breath
vesping outward. Flat Rock is all collision centers
& closed taquerias that morning. After a shower,
I'm not sure what outfit this character would wear. Either:

     1. I'm ordering a scotch after my steak's arrived
     at the White Handshake Country Club

     2. I'm hanging my shirt up, shirtless, on a branch,
     so I can wear it tomorrow, or

     3. My dad asks if I can just run my fingers through
     my hair—at least—before leaving the house
     before he leaves all houses.

THERE'S A CAR WRECK
HERE EVERY DAY. FATAL.
& A NEWS CAST, HERE, EVERY DAY,
ABOUT THE FATAL CAR WRECK.

                        Sometimes things die
          & we throw them in the dirt to grow

more things, replacement things. Sometimes
              we throw dead things into a pan to sizzle,

else we just leave them inside-out on the shoulder.
              Sometimes a siren or newscast or pulsing head

-board drives my attention beyond this box
              to the mawkish precipitation staining the sky

          all the way down. But our eyes are dry, true
dry, waiting for these elevators like upright coffins

to take us to the parking garage.   Days later:
you're sleeping, I hope, & I'm going back for seconds

on free muffins during the active shooter training.

&I suddenly feel very alone.   Days later:

a toddler is a fossil

of the memory of youth & January is Kansas City
thawing to expose the fossil of Kansas City

from November. The Walgreens & Checks Cashed Payday Loans
across the street are alive with the glistening

dyed cotton traffic of convenience & despair
economics. It will get colder again outside

&/or inside these budding winter bodies. I can't predict

the future nor this moment & I can't remember

much except an actual heart beating in my hand

like something I better throw back into the sea

        if I want to give it even half a chance.

IN AN UNEXPECTED
CONSUMER EMERGENCY,
I FIND MYSELF

at a mall, for the first time in years, both a fraction & a multiple,
searching for some compulsory rubbish

for our home until I step outside: some infant rests
in Dead Duck Pose

[all chattering indistinctly]

& airplanes & such
collide, chandeliers sagging the heavens. Later, here we are,

sitting in the shade
of our mail-order tent as the forest rots & collapses,

yet music. The songs we hear coming out from these
dendritic wrecks

are songs we'll never tell. I stutter at the day & here
we are, titanic

[engine starting]

in hesitation,
pedestrian & romantic. Later, my cartoon bride, you & I suddenly

find ourselves
in a hotel, using our inside voices, NSFW. We use ourselves up

trying to try to communicate. The implosions of stars are reruns

on a network
of reruns. So here we are in our suite, robes presenting

in the closet,
the worst of our boxed media flattened & delivered.

We segue, fade out. We jump-cut. Later, here we are, then,
in a state

park cabin, our changeling boy in a melt-pile beside us
in the interior,

[engine sputtering]

in the interior
as above again the inviolable light is projected & projected,

plagiarized,
barked into its own expanding darkness. Later, here we are now

at home.
We'll end up shutting our windows in a storm. You recite

the grounding
exercises; I collect the sharps. Dear everyone else (the world,

the noise), I'm just not here for advice—the sea receding,
the twins

sensing each other, all that shit. There are peaceful periods:
[gun firing]

trials of famous
men, pouty beards by candlelight. Run your fingers through

with me & don't
wash your hands. Let the fields drift slowly by. If you jump

you will land: we're prisoners. Bells ring. They often do. Thick,
audible sucks

of breath. I'm not here. Bells cough, fluttering a new numeral.
Your testament

[some cheers & applause]

qua the waning
color & rallying artifice of this portrait, your thrumping sigh

unmanned
into the elbow crook of my coat cotton. This is your pillow, dear.

This is my goddamned face. Low church. Scurry of coins
across the hard

-wood. Damn it, Lord, I'm resigning to spend time
with my family.

Our early versions
of us, bled of their flush, drift slowly by. Damn it. The Babylonians

invent zero. We drill
for water. Damn it, Lord, if you want to talk, leave a flag in the flower

-pot on the balcony or birdshit on the spire. Julie, you call me
on my day

off to tell me you just saw a ghost. I believe you & don't believe you
& maybe

[people clamoring]

I'm the ghost.
Sky filled with bugs, city of stacked moons, & you, my bride, speak

to a young squirrel
low in a tree as our dog-faced boy eats dirt. You worry. You worry

that your new meds'll make it harder to come, but you just came
twice this second

time this afternoon. I come to in the morning after bad sleep.
You talk

to our dog
-faced boy of the future. I look for any unbroken wine glasses

& just end
up filling a coffee mug for you. You end up crying

[engine sputtering]

& worrying about looking sad & puffy tomorrow. I worry about you
crying or

cutting & squeeze you to sleep.
Later, here we are in a hotel in Omaha. I'm cleaning up

your red wine
fireworks in this bathroom not ours with toilet paper & care.

I'm insisting you drink water. Imploring water. I'm barely there. How often

do I repeat myself? At what point echo avalanche? What'll get you kicked out

of the choir?
Pennies thrown at you.

I want to tune the radio to the new tune, spatchcocked & unpredictable in its news.

I want
less. I turn off baseball & put on some music. I turn off the music

& return to the news.
My sour smurf, this seems untenable. We're goners. But

we're resourceful. We'll find a way through this like an inmate
finding a way

to hang herself. When I start to shave, you towel off my back
& break down.

"What will happen if I'm gone?" you ask. "Who will make sure your
    back is dry?"

Later, I'm chasing you
down Front St. I'm chasing you down Woodland. I'm chasing you down

the empty trail. Our third
is crying in the kitchen. I'm chasing you down Higgins. Down

Pulaski. I'm chasing you down Chestnut, down Irving Park, down
the brown line,

down the long way, down the last years. On occasion I am here.
I watch & breathe

& imagine skies
unbuckling. I exhale & bilge & gulp & imagine or hope. Signal flare.

There were fireworks last night. Oh-uh-oh-uh-oh-uh-oh. Woke up

to a parade in the rain in St. Louis. I found a new wound on my body.
I'll draw

a crooked little crown on each photo I find in any of these boxes. From
the seven

-teenth floor,
I see a man asleep in the bed of a pickup truck in a lot. The rain-dark

surfaces in all visible directions,
horses tether to carriages & line up. Another man is nearly

struck by a car. Your voice hits me instantly & then lingers for a long while, a cat bite

on a knuckle. What do we do with the biographies of our heroes—
the cheap madness

& best-of
compilations? I can't feel myself where your voice hit me; I think

it's infected.
It's ok. Dying young is a rite of passage. Stranded families & sad phone

messages. Searching your eyes for the trademarks of various
pharmaceutical

companies. Small print. Even here. Right now, tonight is darker than it's
been yet tonight.

We take turns,
you first, squatting in the tub: we wash each other

off of ourselves,
though I don't wipe my mouth.

[crowd cheering]

Yesterday, we had $9. In the world. My card got declined
for a 10 under $10

bottle of wine. I thanked the insufferable, sympathetic cashier & left.
Tonight we sweat it out.

The visual
queering. It all opens up. Darkness pumps up the volume. Yet tonight.

Yet the myth
of narrative, progress. Yet tonight the distant dim inhales. Mostly,

I see patterns. Of space. Behaviors in space. Rhythm. A parade. Mostly I see a parade.

REMISSION
INVENTORY

NOVELTY
COUNTRY
SONG

Well, tonight is not the only place I am
tonight. Beyond me & between me
light bulbs hiccup & burble

& a frenzied squirrel loses its map
of maples & restarts. Maybe we ought to
take what we've still got & laminate it in frost

& then salt & then the gold leaf over spring's pat rapture.

There are things I've learned already this young
soft year I don't know what to do with: one
gets a pregnancy test when in the ER

for their attempt on their own life. What to name that baby?

I worry I'm doing this wrong. I've got beans soaking, sharps
& meds hidden, the last dank well swill of our bank account
miraculously transformed into boxed wine. Winter's here

with its expressive eyebrows & doomed neighborhood cats
under every car. You yawn so I kiss you & you taste better
than free food, but you can't sleep & I try to stay up reading

but layers of exhaustion—wet blankets on this piss whisper
of a fire—keep accumulating. I worry you'll do it right next time
& I'm still attached to this day of ours, whatever day it is.

[SIGHING]

I pity those who will never get to see you naked.
I pity you, too, sometimes, for you married a boy.

A white boy. A Rust Belt white boy. It's sleeting
outside & I am outside, part of the landscape.

It's been a long week

we say every week. We've plans to make
plans. I'm walking home to you.

This apology is complicated. My face changes.

I must've scratched my eye or let the left side
of my face sink through the mattress

& into netherlife last night. Can half of me
just see too much now? Am I marked,

a Bell's Palsy, a broken window letting the bees in?

My one eye cries now at the mere day's
discount lighting, so much so that Jean-Ann,

ringing me up at the market, asks if I'm OK.
How do I center this swimming world? How do I answer?

HEARTLAND,
PT. 1

It was my job to create & distribute emotions

or emotional apparatus. I dragged my remnants
of empire across the main drag at dusk. A kiosk.

A shrine. Cenotaph. Another funeral parade,

morning was to be very noisy with failure.

Very human. My job was to analyze the events
at the free concert at Altamont the way others

have done Little Round Top, the Challenger,

or *Our American Cousin*'s spontaneous
intermission. & then, within a haunting's reach

of the palace ruins, I converted. Scratched
my name right into the wall as an impotent doctor

pokes his pinky into the president's living brain. Our team lost.

Iowa is the worst. A car-struck carcass. An audience
-tested, family-friendly adaptation of a beloved song

for a commercial for cough medication. The hell we need.

CHARLOTTE
STREET

New city, city of displaced basement stone & cat shit
  in every yard, your sky is painfully clear.

It leaves me skimming in circles for something else to watch.
  My new city neighbors remind me of everyone I know:

sleeping on the bus, launching their tumblers over the kitchen card
  table, slow dancing in the diner, skimming in circles

until watching their own dizziness.

  Dizzying new city of boredom & sky, your trees
sag their chins, dugs, scrota, tendrils like soggy fries

  in the microwave. The grass on your TVs is awful green.
As crisis actors, we have active sex only after finishing

  the first episode of *The Vietnam War* & hearing of a friend's divorce.
Every night, once the light's off, sirens start up, driving

  in circles.

Nightly, the adaptive repetition: cells & stars & dreams
    of shootings & chandeliers falling & the stampede. If the house

is actually burning, what do I grab? A little slice of flame?
    Julie's busy mice? The last of the bourbon & a handful

of the window's slow-settling liquid? The up-to-code detectors
    are screaming & screaming & sirens are nearing as I try

to choose, as I lie in our bed & cure.

HUNTED
BY
DEAD
ANIMALS

Condemned as we are to this rent, I wake up,
dress in shivers—white paint

over white paint—& leave the light off.
This way it's slower, which is a synonym

for holier in moments of attention. February.

We speak the names of these months tender, like
those of suddenly favorite or suddenly dying children.

When I stop talking I realize how loud I'd been,

an apartment when the whistling heat shuts off.
These neglected dying children, named February

for now, return like holiday sales. I shut up now

for the dead noises resurrected. There are no dreams
where I'm headed—Kansas City, Kansas—so you sleep

for me. You're beautiful, probably. It's dark out, but
my memory's as clear as the interstate at this hour.

ENTELECHY,
NEBRASKA

House cat on the highway, I know you're dead,
but had you just started your way across

or were you almost there? It makes all the difference to me.

My birthday's closing in, again, & I just want to look again
like Harvey Keitel in 1973 & sing like Dolly Parton at age 71,
on the evening of Loretta Lynn's stroke.

I'm wearing a white sleeveless t
& an unbuttoned Nudie Cohn suit top
& saddle shoes & no socks

& a broken nose & a tooth chipped
by an ex's right jab. Dance with me.

There's my curved spine, growing toward the screen,
the progenitor of whatever this is, the official sponsor
of weekday loneliness.

Voice-over explains the context that the image just can't
carry & the director is too scared to cut. I don't see it.

I want it to look again like it does in all of your first family
photographs, era announced by the home décor & haircuts.
I'm aging as I watch this. I'm closer to death than birth, even

if I accept Jesus Christ as my personal doula. Instead, I flip
through the box & await your opening number. Give me something

in a 1977. Announce it with wood paneling & hair
so thoroughly brushed that it'll need to be corrected

with a decade's worth of perms. I'll just sit down
on the tile floor & wait for the screaming.

REMISSION
INVENTORY

.

You crawl into bed with me
in a later scene. "Wake me up!" you wake up

screaming in this earlier scene. Then you sleep
the whole drive back to Des Moines. I wake up

early to drive back alone & slice my finger open
slicing a salt bagel open. Sucking on a Band-Aid

through Missouri towns in sad need of hospice
care, I'm twirling this ring dizzy & humming along

some sad standard. Every standard. One at a time.
I'm with you: a buddy finger taped to a broken one,

if you like. Neither of us is able to bend nor grip nor
do anything much delicate. Tomorrow's a great day

to get pregnant, your phone says. In another indoor world,
a necktie as tourniquet on Love Grove Lane, a towel

as tourniquet on Charlotte Street. In this later scene,
after you swallow them all & crawl into bed, your

Midwestern Boy Husband dressed you—panties & a t
at least—before the EMTs showed up. He locked

the dog in the bedroom, got the keys, got in the car.
For a while, it goes split screen. Back at the House

for Two-Dimensional Male Characters & Bad News,
your Midwestern Boy Husband is a clipped goose

coughing in the yard, a soundtrack searching for its film,
or a space station falling. I'm burning up in re-entry.

I can't look to my right. Passenger side blind, flying
in circles, glazed numb with my overeager gulp

of first coffee, then the tinny disappointment
of a Diet Coke. In another indoor world, we leave

our blinds open, airing to our second-story
neighbors the particulars blurred on network television.

First fly of the season, drunkenly barreling into
the window & the lamp & the blinds, identify

your emergency. Transition. You look at your Midwestern
Boy Husband with his opinions & birthmark & weak

-nesses & his feathers & down bed poorly made. He's in front
of the mirror, saying, "Body of bourgeoning pelican chin

& sad green eyes, where will we be in three years?
In ten? Will we live on these dirty, wrong-lit plains?

Are we at home?" I am not proud of any of this, though
I am too proud. In our neighborhood of burning plastic,

I am always writing you this song. Highly ritualized,
it will be performed in town in pestilence. Eventually,

with volume in my eyes, even as young kindling, I know
what it is to drown. You've taken your prescribed amount

of sleeping pills. I'm late to bed. You've taken your pills
& by the time I get to bed I am rat & swan & shut me up.

Shut me up, dawn—you seem a simple curse. A ritual.
Hospitals & funerals & here I am. Singing out of tune,

which is my key. Guest starring: stock footage of snowstorm,
a disease in debut, & here we are, losing them all to sleep.

Some part of me, the patterned part, expands
as if newly diagnosed. You show up unaccompanied,

like Hazel Dickens singing "Black Lung." I am so sorry
this is all so worrisome & so repetitive. I'm so so sorry

I talk so much. Let me play your body through
its own awareness. You call out Jesus' name, but

end up secular in the bathtub. You grab me by the hair
but end up holding me like a soon-bruised apple. You say the world

is not fair & it's not. People in this town are transporting
stories in vans we can't imagine. Snow's all melting, milk

weaker than the Steve Miller Band but not as white.
Every time, as prelude to seizure, I smell

Thanksgiving stuffing, I smell Ottessa Moshfegh's
My Year of Rest and Relaxation. I smell Denis Johnson's

goddamn human wilderness & back issues of *TV Guide.*
I get up, brush the hair off my pants, & go

to pay rent. The world moves in rosemary & butter
substitute, you say your prayers & do your morning

repetitions, & here I am, pissing in your pool.
This year: a dog that needs to be put down. A mercy.

In another indoor world, perseverance is a man running
up stairs in an otherwise empty stadium with his shirt

off, socks up, over the word Perseverance. In another
indoor world, the president steps out of the shower

& feels old. Since one's not supposed to feel anything
not the feel of a champion, he changes the subject.

He orders an airstrike. He calls for some silk boxers.
In another indoor world, in the Des Moines Art Center,

A Line Made by Walking was made by Richard Long
walking. I've drawn this line up & down

I-35 a dozen times these weeks. I think it was all forest
when your dad started. The first trip, I brought funeral clothes

just in case. There is no immortality. Neighbor Mary
baked him a pie just as soon as he couldn't eat

& isn't that just the way of this goddamn petty world?
As he transitions to object-slash-memory, an inventory:

There was sweat on his scalp, a percolator in his throat.
His eyebrows, his only voice, were singing the sweep

of his morphine dreaming. Our hands stayed his chest
after his breath abandoned, a lost cause, evicted apartment.

Those eyelids closing are only the envoys of a whole,
rounded world lidded & shut down, curtained & closed

for the night. Trucks drive by. You break a glass. This
ending yet to end. In another indoor world, this painting

here has a warped horizon, as if even the surface
of the sky is drying paper turned more outward

than it ought in its yield to the mirroring mocking of the sea.
The embrace—which lasts forever—never lasts long.

AFTER YOU
PATENT
YOUR BLUE

like Yves Klein or Eric Clapton, may the Lord destroy him,
take off your outer layers & walk calmly into the lake,

a lake the size of our main character's hometown, where

farm dogs chase a tourist's car until the headlights die
in the oblivious fogskin nebula.

This is a fiction. Walk it if you can. I'm so thirsty
marching through this hundred years' war, this

thousand-year flood plain, this once in a lifetime event.

Chapter 2 is the name of the inadequate son. He swans
by the river downtown, drinking black water, biting

at garbage. I return to your bed, a raft, a floating grave,
the whoosh of traffic eager as an arrow. Each word

is bleeding out its speaking, though
everyone else is sleeping. My boots

& jeans & old man shirt & inner layers are all pooled
on the floor. I breathe until I too sleep & dream

of all the towers that will bow & simplify these

next centuries. I've no money in my wallet
& so make it mime a coughing fit. A phone rings.

It's the government. It's a special offer from my old area code.
I close my eyes & remind myself, "I have a crush

on Jesus. I only have a crush on Jesus." My phone buzzes.
It could be him. As long as I don't look, it could be anyone.

THE HOOSIER
SEAT

Patrick's leaving for LA—an aspiring
actress, a failing football team.

We talk about how we're talking
about James Hampton again.

How many days exactly are in a while?
Are you adding hours to your life

by switching time zones? A city
can overstay its welcome—its

unforgiving tangle of bad mornings,
Jungle Law billboards, Kansas City's poor

myopic eyes. Patrick Keizer is a smart man
& so plans to burn every standing bridge

into Kansas, to ensure this bus, humming
through Place Name, Colorado, is always & ever only

one way. We all hope to go west & west
until there's no more. To end in water.

We all hope to surprise the survivors

with the meticulously lit skin of our garbage,
gilded when it's long too late.

TAXIDERMY
AS A BRAND
OF DOMESTICITY

Utility workers uncover a grave of limbs
& I blame my coincidental likeness

to persons living & dead & to the thunder
like something dragged over the surface.

I press the bruise, it sings a song,
& a starling screams a child's scream.

The bruise sings
& I love the song so much I grant it

irrevocable power of attorney. A woman
in her fifties in floral print is weaving

around out front, pointing her phone
at the storm, talking about angels.

The storm circles like skin around
a wound, the horizon a video tape in 1992

in need of tracking. I'm singing this song,
sweating through my shirt, bleeding

into the leaves, applying for a Visa
Platinum card. The song eats its own

footprints from the repeating snow
& I already have a headache tomorrow.

Ohia. We make sex to the saddest music
& it's the feel-good story of the summer.

We love to the gutting songs.   O,
lover. O, Whippoorwill.   In this

mechanic's wind, I'm always on the verge.

You break a glass. Diseases wipe out a continent.
The world ignores itself with great skill.

              You break a glass.
              You bring us home.

The wind's supposed to pick up overnight.
We laid together in the entranceway, trying

to sleep, on the couch, trying, on my twin
bed, a slow meal, on your Pilsen bed, still warm

from your girlfriend, fled to some Dakota.

A low revelry, I twaddle & plane like
a child. Flames don't lick or flicker,

they panic like someone themselves pressed to flame.
We're all just saving each other's lives over here.

One follows the other to the bathtub;

one has to let the dog-faced boy out into the winter,

the world bright & cold, silent
& dumb & blinding & still, everywhere.

THE
SECOND
DESCENT

The ground will thaw & freeze & the snow
on top of the mountain will become a heel

stomping the beer can house
at the bottom of the mountain. Five cent refund.

So shall I be disfigured.

Light will nibble at the surface of the winter
's river then slow under cloud cover, giving up,

then petrify from silver into shadow
then blinding then blind.

Dramatic slow-mo shot with lens cap on.

They're killing Barnum & Bailey, the last man
on the moon. A man with a prop Bible

approaches the corpses.

There is no dramatic breeze left
for your elephant graveyard.

We're so bored that we're overshot
back to sober. This voice is always stuck

in my monologue like the Gideon's Bible
in the bedside drawer of some hotel room

we only rented for the sex. I believe.

                              I believe the infirm

will not dance again, though we'll dress them
in their best at the end. To make this all

a tent revival—a re-pastoral—you'll paint
the bloated corpses as models of sleep.

I'll sell the catastrophic horizon as sunset.

HEARTLAND, PT. 2

In credits, now, you'll see me as Chubby Girl, Smoking
Teen #3, Trans-Neptunian Object, Middle Child.
I'm singing into the tines at the end of my own
stolen silver (like it's a microphone)

my poleaxed boatsong—unhaunted & full of gasoline
—all from the corrugated bed of an American pickup.

Inside, bleach water starts down through the ceiling
of our closet. We rush our boxes of photos & letters
& naked drawings of each other & others. Paralyzed.
Time lapse. Silver spit of wear shimmying

the foreground. Scratch your name into the wall,
your flag into the surface. Collaborate
with me. We can cancel each other out,
cancer the benign parade of signals

across the careful sea. Plainchant, restrictions apply.*
It is my job to collect objects, to try to explain
to my father the words of my mother, to my mother
the phases of eclipse. Inside, I am praying

for my sports team or loved one's recovery as you
masturbate in the bathtub. Real people. Not actors.
Carelessly, in prayer, I toss a name, a placenta,
a water balloon. Baptism! Baptism! Baptism! Bah!

[DOOR
SLAMMING]

There's a horse on the roof in a flood. We used to drive
for nights & smoke to keep busy & awake. The peristyle.
It's all getting a little too easy.

Like a war photographer, you just stand there.
Like a war, it continues. I'm just in this
for the exit strategy.

Later, on the banks of the old bathtub, I watch you
breech like a sexy whale. Let it be shown
that in this metaphor

I am also a whale, but one sitting on a toilet, while you,
toweling off now, are ready to sit
on ceremony's face.

I'm just in it for the exit interview. Later,
there's a hole that you nailed in the wall
along a pencil line

you drew to aim the hole. Whatever was hanging
is boxed up, thrown away
or at the Goodwill.

The hole looks like a smoochy face, a trumpeting anus,
a president's mouth, a propellered plane
swooping in to our bucolic

countryside. This is how we say goodbye to Iowa.

[DRAMATIC
MUSIC
CONTINUES]

You looked at me, sure, but you were an office building
downtown with 2/3 of the lights off at 10:30 pm,

janitors dragging mop buckets along
behind your eyes. You loved me in the daylight,

but the garage is nearly empty at this hour.

Audience sits quiet & orderly as a plague pit
& everyone's coughing as if we just copyrighted shame.

You've written me one thousand sweet notes
& I don't deserve you. All of my saved voice

messages are love & song & dying friends &—
by definition—the past. I listen, sometimes

—twice a year maybe—& delete a few
each time. Then I start a fire.

Someone's rubbing oil on someone else's head
& there are cats everywhere. Dude

looking like a Chuck Close self-portrait
plays a twelve-string & sings of time

& shame & his mother & death & such.

Now I have oil on my head. Mia kissed me
on the top of this head & now there's glitter.

Why clap, flesh echo, world falling on world? Ashes
in the Ganges. Mike is on the front porch yelling,

"Customer service!" into his phone

with an increasingly angry delivery. We drove to Warrensburg
to get vaccinated in a church full of National Guard troops.

After I change Lou in the back seat, we pass
three more churches, a dead airplane, a worship center—

which is different—& the lengthening

days' transition lightscape. "Customer
service, motherfucker!" When the only plan

is surrender, meet me in a dream in the alley
with a carton of cigarettes, monks starching with egg whites.

THE
ANSWER

This child-sized raccoon just casually scaled that entire maple,
slow as a professional sunset.

Mallick light gets sleepy, gets sticky, & congeals.

Minnesota is not the answer. There's no way lakes lie
like that lake lies nightly. Awake & alone,

I'm sitting here sleepy as a Kennedy on Nantucket,

waves groping at the nearest shore. 13,314 twilights
not the answer. That sound in the increasing darkness

over there is sleep spreading out & checking its net—
or a grazed deer limping—or a set piece falling.

Spotlights, oncoming headlights, not the answer.
This is a song called "Oncoming Headlights

Are Not the Answer." This is the song I sing
until it's over. Until it's done. Until it's sung. Until the crash.

It's been a long night & your mouth already tasted like rain. Writing
often of the sky instead of tasting it, I look to the sconces & the sconces
look fake & their light looks fake & I have authentic responses to both,
which is how storms start. As seasons

digest themselves (a short talk on short talks), holiday cards become
less applicable & so more affordable & Fox 8 or whatever news vans
circle some immanent site of tragedy tourism. Some nights I go out & walk
the sidewalk in socks or bare feet

longer than I'd meant to & notice the crystal glass & homely bends
& feel deeply the Troost neighborhood. My ears circle in on themselves,
stereo sinkholes. I'm eavesdropping & I'm sorry. I've had bad teeth forever
& so got online & bought God's vibrator

as a toothbrush & stood before the middle-aged self's mirror.
White as I am, I trust most the islands that kill their first tourists.
A cargo ship full of luxury cars continues to burn in the Atlantic.
A mother about a mile from right here

killed her dog & decapitated her son after calling the cops on the devil.
The snows. Rubble-crusted outskirts of Kiev. The soft snoring
of our toddler. What do we do? I dither. I stand numb before the light.
                    I look deeply. I look like Fabio

if, instead of an angular chin, his face flesh just dangled & then if also
that formless dangle carried on down the rest of the frame. My point is
I have long hair right now. A Hadean earth. A thought floating in
                    like pickled nimbus, ghost fart. In the mirror,

I am my middle school self making muscles at himself, waiting
for hair to grow, SCUD missiles arcing across the nightly news
downstairs. Tonight, I got news off Facebook, so already sad.
When I found out Robert died, I didn't wake you up. I
                    didn't even check you were asleep. You needed

a night & this news is not the night you needed. The still
-lengthening night repeats. I rarely call in favors, & every
time I do, I claim to do it rarely, but still, please sleep. Go to sleep or
keep sleeping. He was thirty-three. It's later still & your mouth is full
                    of rain. I'll tell you in the morning.

THE
SHALLOWS

This is not about absence. You're here
& you're enormous. You're no math,

but the numbers are swelling. Everything
's a code: the flowers & the blood & the search

engine, the nipple vortex, cancer, horde-swarm,
Sears catalogue, the Third Remove, the scabby

daybreak, the scars, the wrists, the rest, ghost
towns in the backgrounds. Bearded men weep

on a summit. Flannel hugs & a chorus pure:
this is mostly empty space. You're no match.

Evening, & I'm chewing on its used breath
in my emptying infancy. We take it apart

in the dark. Everyone looks the same.
Someone says, "I hate this goddamn river."

Trains sound as we finish our relatively hetero
-normative sexual encounters. Decoupled, maybe

we'll return upstream to our polite, Midwestern
depressions just to dive & reseed our bad ideas,

prodigal spawn of the lazy gospels. It takes so long
for articles of darkness to organize & scavenge

and convince the dim to sing inward its harmonics.
It takes thousands of generations for eyes to be lost.

THE
SINGING
EAR

YOU SAY
MOSQUITO

Never told you I found a dead squirrel & pulled its tail off.
Davy Fucking Crockett. Never told you about Chaplin's corpse.

I did tell you I climbed on the roof & watched *Steel Magnolias*
on a shitty box TV with Lana as Chicago went numb

in its own replacement light. There's no etc.,
its drone done. My grandpa stroked out of words & lying

on our couch with bricks for legs. He used to make me look
in the mirror when I was young & crying. That's me, four years old,

saying, "You look so cute when you cry." Women, please don't show up
in the first five minutes of a murder mystery. Men are the worst.

Men are the worst & please like & share. I come back with my face
a mess. This is how the terrorists win. I'm what's wrong with America.

Burning hospital bills in our tiny barbecue pit in the rain, folding
an infant's onesies at the dining room table, I get a text from Julie

saying, "I miss you," & a text from Verizon saying our bill of $149.76
is due tomorrow. Hand-me-down dinosaurs & mouse-sized socks.

I miss you, too. 149/86 after ultrasound & moving about. 4:00 p.m.
7/16. Stop signs. The secondary market on fake Lincoln letters. Stop signs.

A body in the shallows. Hospital bills. Neil Young in a leather jacket.
A fire extinguisher in the capitol. A costume laugh, a rhetoric.

Are you having trouble / viewing this email / staying asleep /
keeping it down? Ten weeks, looking down at the whirling

sworl of a forming storm on a rapidly developing system,
already named. I Google myself & wander until an obituary

that's almost exactly my name. You Say Mosquito.
Ed shows up for Dad's funeral in a sling & slips me

a twenty, telling me to buy the two biggest cheapest bottles
of Moscato—for real, I like the shitty stuff more. The cousins

in town from New York watch us all smoking in a circle
by the curb. We're the trashy family, but this is what

sorrow looks like here: the piles of photographs. The dozens
of flies. After playing Humpy's birthday, we were invited

to open up for Live Lady Meatfuck at a Flathead reservation bar,
part of probably my favorite drive in America, over the Missions.

Embedded in its opposite, I-70 in Missouri, glows some haggard
trucker lonesome boner warehouse. I tried to cry tonight.

Letting a faucet drip in the winter. My uncanny mess in the mirror
delicate & creepy as squirrel prints in the snow out the side door.

Are you having trouble? Already named, I Google myself.
I'd been told Googling oneself would turn oneself blind.

Blind Gary Davis came to me in a dream. Blind Gary Davis
turned me into a tree. I blind out & see the future. Across the street

from your mom's house, the church & its ringing bells broadcast
through belfry speakers. I put my glasses on even with nothing to see.

HEARTLAND,
PT. 3

Inside, you are busy diagnosing yourself on Wikipedia
as I run my guitar-hardened claws

through my senseless hair & I decide

to pander to my base. I proclaim,
"Sic semper tyrannis!" & jump

from the mattress, nearly break my leg.
I record the incident. The pages pressed against

themselves make the call of embers grayed
by graying waters. Shhhhhhhhhhhhhh

& on & on. "I can hear you writing," you say.
                                    I say,

"I'm sorry." The whisper, this pen,
this thespian flair. This flowering weed

wends up over the way to the scar horizon
where my patrician smile once bent

the light. Steam spills from your talking face,

an underwater wound. We cut to cure. Why bother
changing clothes if we're going to war?

UNDER THE
NANCY GRACE
OF WEATHER

You're reading a book on Jim Jones. Tomorrow, you are forty-seven.
Today, you are 5'1 ¾", Jewish or nothing, combing the shore for fossils.

Watching you, I am 5'10", an atheist Personist. You have tinnitus,
metallic tree crickets in devil stereo. Nothing works & here we are.

The last leaves dangle & shiver, dull orange endangered bats
about to die in their sleep & crowd the ground with their rhyming
    corpses.

You're trying to locate the exact pitch & pulse of your cricket possession.
You're a radio not quite in tune. I'm foil around the tip. There's lightning
    beyond.

Thirty years earlier, I'm sitting on the beer cans in my neighbor's
back seat, the decades' precursor to you saying, "I always loved you;

it's not your fault," as you drove off to do whatever. I jumped in
the passenger window you'd lowered to say good-bye & you drove off,

closing the window on me. Cull. A remix: man beats dog with a stick,
the dog's pads beat the concrete in retreat. I open the book to Job.

I open the book one hundred times & always open to Job. Later, you
   pick at rocks creekside & I write of you picking creekside at rocks.
   I'm spoiled. We've been here—

precisely here—many times. & we've never been here. You return
with a hog-nosed rock, some fossils, these scraps written at you, from
   the memory

of the ecosphere of Big Marty's back seat, nothing changed. Like
   kitchen sink to fruit flies, my gray brain this week attracts an
   opportunistic & minor storm. Waving them away, I hope

to remain mysterious as a left boot & lumpy contractor's bag
on the shoulder of 71 in the empty weight of rush hour. What manner

of carcass am I? Do I warrant a shovel or hose or a vulture's sky burial?
The buzzard vomiting before take-off just reminds me again of you

(Dramamine, swallowing it all back down on the El), then of us (it is
resourceful & familiar, employing our exit strategy from these last few
   towns).

This is pain specific to extraction: gingerly digging a bullet out
with a flame-warshed knife, wiping it off on a gospel of the beauty
   industry,

spitting three times. I nod my head (its inner fecund nest beating
220 times a minute) instead of passing out until I pass out.

I let the dog sleep on your pillow while you're locked in the psych ward.
    I hate this.

I only notice these windows when the lights are out & they try—friend
    of a friend—to balance the night & me looking to it lovely &
    heartbreakingly sweet as this dinner

alone in a cafeteria. Sad & dear as this grilled cheese for one, hospital
vending machine lunch for one, this breakfast from QuikTrip on the
    way home,

for one, tired & happy & worried & supremely present, for once, in
    this bad idea breakfast burrito, the highest form of art, marred &
    barcoded & bound to end

at least a slight disaster. Front desk nurse can't help that he smiles
like a pervert, nor that the Main St., USA streetscape through yonder

ground floor window brings out the plaster in the glim of his half-gaze.
To talk to him is to fall down carpeted stairs, to stick a jayfeather

behind each ear then jump off the roof. I've nothing to tell you. Still, we spoon. We collapse as one. Only as many shadows as lights we forgot to turn off.

As the days carry, sometimes the walls look like meat. Sometimes I'm dead & so hide from our bills just to feel hunted. Then another month is over. Thank God.

We may have lost the battle, but we
also lost the war, & we may have lost
the election & not won the lottery, but

at least each trinket littered in the ditch
is a missive & at least there's choreography
in this traffic dodging the man in crisis

on the exit ramp. Where do you look
for your news? We made ourselves
a little altar & almost set the shrine

on fire. Kneeling in the woods, the audience
is shaking for no good reason. "'Listen!'
I say instead of listening," I say in my play.

In my play, these are the words I say
to the corpse on stage. I've witnessed
real death & pay my way breath by breath.

If none of this means anything, then let's
make every startled syllable drag. The play
is called *The Promise of Heaven*

Is a Pyramid Scheme & I've never
written it. Still, I read it out loud
to the people on the horizon. I've known

them so long I forget their names, which
complicates my ethos. In the next scene,
the entire apparatus ready for floating

is thrown overboard. Act Three: you
scream yourself awake screaming, "You
didn't tell me?!" He turns himself

into a bear, a limping dog, a matted
wolf, a synonym for fur. & then breath
takes over your breath, breath by breath.
Act Four: I name my son Happiness
& send him to his room. I buy him
a present for all of his missed birthdays

& it's crawling with ants. As a kid
on Bellevue, rats ran through my room.
Dad & Ed put up fluorescent lighting

& shower curtains as walls. The floor
took on water & so the carpets mold.
I loved it. I lived in an abandoned

convenience store & it was good
preparation. This was Act One, or
whatever the first part is called.

The world is open twenty-four hours
& does not mean you well, though
it's a place to piss when you need one.

ST. FONTANELLE

Damn it, thirty-six degrees, what do I do
with you, with your trimmed beard
& reasonable shoes, your indecision
& multiple credit cards in your father's
name? Beer bottle shrines like
the Pepsi cups on Freddie Mercury's piano?

As the CIA tries to harness lightning,
flood lamps shock the screen so bright it's empty.
Fragile white America's skull
is all soft spot—a velvet bust. Ad absurdum.

Due to disagreeable weather conditions,
I thoughtfully invite her into my kitchen.
My dad throws ice at the squirrels.
On some unhearable frequency, some unbearable grate.
I trust this place as much as I trust someone
who describes themselves as an entrepreneur.

Inveigled. Indoors, in clothes, & so much sky untroubled.
We got the bloodwork results yesterday
as I was roasting cut nubs of carrots & harissa. When we all shut up
& try to think, sleep is a game I am losing.

HAMBER DESCANT,
A SINGLE ENTENDRE

On the George Brett Superhighway, doe heads point
due South. We want our heroes to be humans.
When Maury showed up with her Tinder date
at the memorial service, I was proud of her. I felt old.
To whelve is to bury deep & there's no such place as heaven.
                                    Offstage, a toilet flushes.

A neighbor's '80s truck is stuck in the mud
in the yard, spinning its smoke. When the dog
            wakes me up @ 1:38, puking, he barfs
like a human. I hold his ears. It's almost a scream.
Julie comes to check on me. It was the middle
of March, 2020, & something new was starting.

It's one of those nights. Dudes scanning the yard
with flashlights turn out to be lightning bugs.
What are we supposed to do
with ourselves? Eventually, by revving forward
he dislodges the tire & arcs through the yard.
It's quiet now, save for the sirens

& my textured breaths, sipping from a thrift store coffee cup—
The Donut King—nodding along to what no one said
or heard. A correction coming. American robins,
            invisible in their ubiquity, beautiful
in their invisibility, shit off of secondary branches

as storms approach from just over there

as Eddie from Brooklyn yells, "Tell her it's Eddie from Brooklyn!"
walking a black mass of panting, knotted shrubbery
                    down Virginia, otherwise abandoned.
I read the shadows the wrong way, not as things
projected by things, not from a surprising place—

like my friend who outed himself / to himself
with his feelings for Judge Reinhold—but just as.
Here we are, smashed souvenir pennies with seasonal disorders
            & sheep's heads, whole. Eddie from Brooklyn
     seems like he calls his ex a whore. All of them. He seems like
he'll insist they were all crazy. Storms approach from just over there.

The Elkhorn is low; the ship stuck, naked, to fill
the canal. Frass. Pleach. Sheep teeth fed into the chief's mouth. Here,
I am your typical missing adult & I like your typical orange shirt,
but have you not seen *Branded to Kill*? The best way for one to act
                    as if on fire is for one to truly be on fire.
                    I'm here to worship in the meddle,

                    to pray for the strange body
               snoring in my bed. Here, one
breaks the toes & tapes them together & walks on, stumbling
          to shut windows during the storm, limping
     to the stringtowns full of loggers

sucking from a wound. To be followed:

                leave a hand-written note, dated or no,

no envelope, proclaiming: "Here, 64% of Americans report an over

-whelming desire to piss in the ocean now we're locked inside,"

imploring, "Go put on a shirt, kid. Learn how to swim.

    If this plane goes down,

                            how do we pronounce your name?"

DEAR FLOOR,
I AM FALLING

for Skoog

This expensive dog the color of a pitted-out white button-down
barks at I suppose the grass. "Ma'am, I've named your Bichon Frisé
First World Problems." I can't stop repeating myself, an analogue

tape loop, a prog rock riff, my excuses ornate as a fall-down bus station
's tin ceiling pressed in a time of boom. My attention pushes me around
like a shopping cart & the afternoon takes a turn, like Cindy

asking me out to lunch & then propositioning me with a nutraceutical
pyramid scheme. People used to say I looked like Jake Gyllenhaal
or the guy from *Shameless* or at least my brother; now they just ask

if I'm ok. I haven't prayed in twenty-seven years, just barely long enough
for my lack of faith to blossom & die at the height of its popularity.
Tonight, what I don't pray for are our recently dead. Rather, it's the mess

they left behind. When left behind, I hope that my image is used to sell shit
that people don't want or need but maybe deserve. Yes, it's the same
Cindy from earlier. Yes, Ed is done with dog poems. Dear Floor,

you're a car that's all headlights. Last night was empty orchestra night
at the Uptown & my morning throat's a littered dance floor
of gin & Bowie. This is a one-lane bridge. Dear Floor, let's be adults

about this. The Mississippi's the color of a puddle from an overnight
flash flood pooled inside a corpse stuffed into a rusty shed. A rock drops
in & scoops a hole charming as the shape of a mouth singing the
    national anthem.

*HEARTLAND
RESTRICTIONS

Not valid if no one shows up, neither in the event that I'm mauled to death on camera, Tin Spill. A tree falls as the currency. Top eyelids. Timber, S.S. Lana Turner! An hour into making love, my employee mind takes over. I worry that you are a secret shopper. Then my mind drifts to gun policy, Syria. You taste real enough, Silver. Moon Landing. What's your biggest fear? Attacked by the sky itself. Face to face if it were a face. Uncontacted tribes stare in horror at the drones approaching. Battleship Sublime, I get giggly. I smell sulfur. I walk out of the interview.

JOSH TREE

Ask the internet, "When does the baby stop
pulling all the Sylvia Plath off the shelves
& keening in mono? When is the mind
no longer three careening flies?" Make the noise
of an angry door opening. I'm here
digging up Gram Parsons. Charlie Chaplin.
I've been downstate putting some meat on
these bones before heading to the coast,
where my porn name is Lester Bangs
& the orphanage of stars is—so far—
uncolonized by saints. My dad is still throwing ice
at the squirrels while I'm jumping through
a cake in "November Rain." Why is your face
making that face? Everyone buries secrets
by dying. Blind Willie Johnson rounding
in space, I find a note I wrote fifteen years ago
while eating a roiling storm bowl of miso soup alone
in Chicago: "Someone will love me again someday
& I'll miss this sort of wasted afternoon."

IN A DOUBLE-WIDE
WITH A SULF'ROUS WELL,
I WROTE MY SON A SONG
for Elizabeth Robinson

Outside of Clinton, MO—a place I recommend
      being outside of—I was
      paying much attention—reverential, really—

to a mattress skeleton, inside a shanty skeleton

      (an echo of the Body Worlds
prenatal room). Leaving, we sprung

      a great blue as we walked
from the stream.
When the world has stopped

      ending, I'll sing you the ingenuous song. A shy dinosaur
startled into grace.

I'm trying to pit my boy against white dude grievance, but I myself
occasionally feel angry as a pickup reversing down a one-way alley.

      Lucien, turn down your radio,
hook your arm over the empty passenger

head rest, & ease out of your mistake.
Months earlier, he was a poppyseed growing.

Then the size of a kidney bean. We paint a room

a new color, Julie assembles some furniture.
I take a vividness of visual imagery questionnaire.

You affect an effect. Apparently, now, a grape.

Our proto-precursors slurried onto the wet bank
with the sound of Julie eating a mango.

I'm making a list of names. Then the size
of an avocado. You affect an effect. You

present a present. You affect an effect. You present

numinous sounds of desperate laughter. An effect.
A plane into a cirrus sets the car alarms keening.

I'm sorry, whose story is this? How long was I asleep?
An affect. Matt is an actor who yells at the TV & makes
things better. A present. I'm singing at you in your allergy.

Aphantasiacs, the picture you can't see is an epic.
The size of a bell pepper. If you speak its language, listen.

THE FIRST
DESCENT

Mick Jagger in *Fitzcarraldo*; our upstairs neighbor's
footsteps; some automation, the wind's machinery:
it all crashes together, waving white caps, frothing.

This sickness, whatever we call it, brands me.

Caruso spins round under a sewing needle
& my breath whistles through my trainwreck
of a nose—this whole organism at war.

Hang on. I can only see the outline of your hair
by candlelight, but hang on. Baby, we're going
to drag our boat over this goddamned mountain.

This is ultimately the end. I brought an apple
& a knife. It never makes the news.

I looked at the pattern on our sofa couch for the first time
tonight. It doesn't really make all that much sense.

I'm codifying my symbols & beliefs

as they're shooting mourning doves on the Travel Channel
or I'm brushing my teeth then spitting out ants
into our rental sink or the president's son

on a river is loading a weapon. I believe in the world,

which never makes the news. An ant cascades over
my wrist & I'm tired. Somewhere, a pregnant woman
is pissing her pants. You break a glass. A sports star

thanks God, commercials charging the gate.
Ants everywhere on the bathroom floor, & the announcer says,
"What a wonderful moment." We raise our Pernod.

Water thrown into the sky; we call it cloud.
                                        A father

tried to drown his little girl on the North Side this week.
Down south, the drizzle pours its loblolly whispers
into my ears & there is interior damage.

"Summer Is a State of Mind" is a cheap poster
plastered on the unwashed wall of my skull,

so I perform a road trip.   Buttoned-up gas stop towns
dutifully zip by.   The porn barns blink slowly.
We're just here for the sloppy miracles. Out of the car,

I find two feathers & two orphaned family photographs.
    Step carefully
& it's a dance. Throw your bottle at the clouds & call it a toast.

Our room tonight is a network of lights. A string of bulbs—
which I write by—strung to altar our bed I write on. Your noise
when you blow out the candle is an airplane. Your click when you

turn off the desk lamp is a snap. You are a machine & a magician.
When you sleep, a campfire burns
& I hear two hundred cracking knuckles, windows, bulbs, necks.

There are fireworks you can't even see, this sleep of yours a ruin.
You wake up screaming. You break a glass. We sleep silently for minutes

or years at a time. Roll over. Harvest the sheet cover into an unstable
landscape
that warns off all but medicated sleep. You breathe in & hold it like a
secret

you're going to have to share
eventually.

GREENOUGH PARK
[WATER SLOSHING]

Earlier, Tim Rakel called & said there's a piano
in the rain in the alley by the church, so then

I'm in the back of a pickup bracing a piano
that may as well be a Tom Waits lyric.

Later, the muezzin in Sarajevo is a recording
& I love him. The children play soccer

in the ruins on the hilltop under night's red
leathery head over the fossil of the library.

Earlier, at the group home, I'm trying
not to get punched by Roger

when you call. I walk out
onto the driveway & try

to fake calm & keep you
on the phone & I quit my job

on the spot & drive to the river
to find you. A train that derails

still arrives at a destination, each wall
of trees & each hummock sloping to underpass

a ghost terminus. Later, scanning through the AM band
on the hour: Cattle machinery. Sports Radio 810. Jesus.

Flood victims. Wildfires. 8th inning. The ministry. Earlier,
after you gave me the first skinny kitchen knife, I threw it

over the fence & onto the roof of one of the hundred
storage units next door. Let someone else find it. Later:

ranchero ballad horn section. The studio audience. Country
Jesus harmony. I'm your host. Fight of the Century. Earlier,

from the river, you got back in the car with me. I slipped
the second skinny kitchen knife in the driver's door pocket,

between CDs & candy wrappers & the abandoned coat
of our dog-faced boy. You made me promise not to read

the note when we got home. Later, back in this dumb Mid
-western town, these empty highways bleed the city back out

into the hummocks on the horizon, heavy in concentrated light.
I'm watching them try. I'm trying, too, but can't stand to watch.

Rain on the windows sounds like mice
on their wheel. The world's song

has become noise, but not like Eno
or Thurston Moore or Rachel's
or Cage noise—like wet mouse noise,

like one whose ear starts to sing.
The twenty-first century gets darker but never

dark. Sleepy but never asleep. Asleep
but never sober. "I haven't slept," I whisper

to you through the rodent noise of your
tinnitus. "The twenty-first century
is a singing ear."

[GLASS
BREAKING]

Sitting there with buzzers in your hands—
        like draining a cyst, like emptying out

        a dictator's bank account—
your plaid gown grows as you shrink.

Naming your enemies, consider the plasticity of the brain as the sky
    falls,

letting something in to help you let
something out. It helps. You gather everything

you have left & all it is is a breath & all it is
is a breath that is all you need.

The night never quite equitable, I always want more.
Always tired tomorrow.

I stay up reading endless fiction
while you dream

& kick & scream & sigh, rolling under our blankets
as under tides.

You've a scar on your knee from your first time
in the ocean.

I took you there.

ACKNOWLEDGMENTS,
THANK YOU,
I MISS YOU,
ETC.

Thanks to the editors and readers of these journals and projects that took versions of some of this:

Another Chicago Magazine: "Our Room Tonight Is a Network"
Bear Review: "[inaudible question]," "The Second Descent," "Dear Floor, I Am Falling"
BOAAT: "Heartland Restrictions"
Court Green: "Entelechy, Nebraska," "The Answer"
Painted Bride Quarterly: "Benesh," "Pneuma," "Novelty Country Song," "You Say Mosquito"
Sixth Finch: "Heartland, pt. 1," "Greenough Park [water sloshing]"
Sprung Formal: "But Little to Say," "[screen image simulated]," "After You Patent Your Blue," "Magnitude Explained," "Under the Nancy Grace of Weather"
Third Coast: "The Shallows"

And so many thanks thanks thanks to the friends, family, and other weirdos who've been here on the way. (I tried to be frugal and constrained in my thanks for the first book. Never again!)

To wit:

The Soloy and Soloy-adjacents: Ma, Sara and Curt, Eric and Lauren; and the Rouse-Brown-Kallestads: Barbara, Jenny, Bill, Sophie, Owen, Seth, and Claire.

To the fabulous poets and readers and friends who've helped me on these poems (and others) over the last many years, particularly: Andrew and Laura (hi, Sandro!), Philip and Natalie, Arielle Greenberg, Ed Roberson, Suzanne Buffam, David Trinidad, Lisa Fishman, Bob Baker, Elizabeth Robinson, Ed Skoog, Khaty Xiong, Jason Sommer, Jordan Stempleman, Marcus Myers, Karen Volkmann, Colin and Rachel, Debra Magpie Earling, Gates.

Such thanks to Diane Goettel and the whole Black Lawrence family. From phone calls and dinner to readings and edits, I've gotten somehow more familiar with my own work and the work of some fabulous writers. The support is truly appreciated.

The St. Louisans: Sean Semones, Paul Lodes, Tim Rakel, Josh and Micaela, Chris and Melissa, Dave Bailey, then Dale, Dalton, Marcus, Mort, and the whole sick Tivoli Crew, plus the old KDHX.

On location in Kansas City: Kate Melles and the Blue River folks; Natalie, Andy, Jennifer and the KCAI kids; Reed, Mark, Kendall, and the other Chez Charlie dirtbags; Simon, Megan Kaminski, Sabrina, Angie, Samantha, Julian, Lauren and Henry.

Des Moines: DMACC, the writing lab unit, whoever shows up at the Dam, Rogan, Sharon and Austin, Ashley and the other former scratching posts.

Missoula: Mackenzie, Brett (a big boy who don't open for nobody!), Henrietta Goodman, Emma Torzs, everyone I got to run into in Portland, Rachels Petek, Mindell, the band Rachel's, any other Rachels, Sparkle Laundry.

Chicago: Dave Becan, Becca Klaver, Danimal and Matt Larson and the Century sentry, our exes, the band I played with in the carriage house Colin lived in, our CTA cards.

Lawrence: Johnny and Rachel, Cody and April, Jo Davis-McElligott, Jimmy, Charlie, that one woman who invited us to a house party where Will Oldham showed up in his tour van.

In all the busking, workshopping, line cooking, projectionist work, reading, teaching, cat wrangling, moving, laundering, and living, I've been buried with big people in small moments that stuck. Thanks, yo.

Thanks to libraries. No thanks to Eric Clapton. Piece of shit.

BJ SOLOY is the author of *Our Pornography &
other disaster songs* (winner of Slope Editions Book
Prize) and the chapbook *Selected Letters* (2016, New
Michigan Press). He teaches at a community college
and persists in Des Moines, home of the whatever.